# Elementary Logic

## Michael de Villiers

Second Edition                    December 2011

First published by the Research Unit for Mathematics
Education at the University of Stellenbosch (RUMEUS)
in 1987, and republished here with permission.

**Dynamic
Mathematics
Learning**

© 2011 Michael de Villiers (trading as *Dynamic Mathematics Learning*)

ISBN 978-1-105-32069-9

# Errata Addenda

p. (i)      Last line: George Boole (1815 – 1864)

p. (ii)     Third last line: Mathematics and logic are identical ...

p. 2        Ninth line from bottom: in everyday life

p. 14       Twelfth line from bottom: $p => q$.

p. 24       Problem no. 4: Respective Tops of Third and Fourth Columns:

$$\overline{p} \; ; \overline{q}$$

p. 35       Last word: premise

p. 36       Third last line: $a <=> b$ is true

p. 48       Twelfth line from the top: description

p. 51       Eleventh line from the top: $\left[ \overline{p} \Rightarrow (q\,\overline{q}) \right] \Leftrightarrow p$

p. 52       Sixth line from the bottom: $\left[ p\,\overline{q} \Rightarrow r.\overline{r} \right] \Leftrightarrow (p \Rightarrow q)$

p. 71       Eleventh line from the top: premises

p. 74       Thirteenth line from the bottom: premises

p. 86       Sixth line from the bottom: $\sin x = 0$ or $\sin x = \frac{1}{2}$

**Dynamic
Mathematics
Learning**

ISBN 978-1-105-32069-9

"I can never bring you to realize the importance of sleeves, the suggestiveness of thumbnails, or the great issues that may hang from a bootlace." - Sherlock Holmes in Sir Arthur Conan Doyle's "A case of identity"


"'Contrariwise', continued Tweedledee, 'if it was so, it might be; and if it were so, it would be: but as it isn't, it ain't. That's logic'." - From Lewis Carroll's "Alice Through the Looking-Glass"


"Assuming there is a reliable method of argument which can be learned, it would be a sorry business if a man, because he has met with some of those arguments, were not to blame himself or his own lack of skills, but were to end in vexation by choosing to throw the blame upon the arguments, and were to hate and ridicule them for the rest of his life, and be deprived of the truth, i.e. the knowledge of reality." - Socrates in Plato's "Trial and Death of Socrates"


"Logic is the hygiene which the mathematician practices to keep his ideas healthy and strong." - Hermann Weyl


"The supreme triumph of reason is to cast doubt on its own validity." - Miguel de Unamuno

# TABLE OF CONTENTS

# PREFACE

"The human race, considered in relation to its
own welfare, seems comparable to a battalion
that marches in confusion in the darkness,
without a leader, without order, without any
signal or command to regulate its march, and
without any attempt on the part of individuals
to take cognizance of one another. Instead of
joining hands to guide ourselves and make sure
of the road, we humans run hither and yon, and
merely interfere with one another."

Words of the Pope or another religious leader? Or perhaps a political organization or the United Nations? No,
these words were already written three hundred years ago
by Leibniz (1666), who believed that the ultimate pana-
cea for the lack of human co-operation lay in the formulation of a universal language and an algebra of reasoning. Although this view of Leibniz was surely naive, he
can nevertheless be viewed as the founder of modern
logic. Whereas the old Greeks did not make much progress
with their study of Logic due to their lack of a
meaningful symbolic system, Leibniz could algebraically
symbolize the laws of logic. (It must be remembered that
Leibniz was a (younger) contemporary of Descartes (1637)
who, despite his notable contributions in analytic geometry, is also viewed as the father of modern algebraic
symbolism (e.g. $y = ax^2 + bx + c$)).

Important contributions to Logic was furthermore made by
George Boole (1854), Augusté de Morgan (1806-1871),

Guiseppe Peano (1858-1932) and Gottlieb Frege (1848-
1925). At this stage logic was expanded considerably to
include all the forms of reasoning which appear in
mathematics. In fact, several mathematicians began to
believe that logic could provide a sound foundation for
the whole of mathematics, as well as to guarantee the
necessary rigor for the resolution of certain paradoxes
which plagued mathematics at the turn of the nineteenth
century. These ideas culminated in Bertrand Russell and
Alfred North Whitehead's monumental work of 1910-1913,
"Principia Mathematica". In this work mathematics is
viewed merely as a natural extension of the laws and
subject matter of logic: mathematics is thus seen as
identical to logic; or as one of its subsets. Russell,
for example, explained their findings in the "Principia"
as follows:

> "The proof of this identity (of mathematics and
> logic) is, of course, a matter of detail; star
> ting with premises which would be universally
> admitted to belong to logic and arriving at re-
> sults which as obviously belong to mathematics,
> we find there is no point at which a sharp line
> can be drawn with logic to the left and
> mathematics to the right. If there are still
> those who do not admit the identity of logic
> and mathematics, we may challenge them to
> indicate at what point, in the successive
> definitions and deductions of Principia
> Mathematica, they consider that logic ends and
> mathematics begins."

This view that mathematics and logic is identical, has
ever since endured fierce criticism from other prominent
mathematicians like Henry Poincaré, Felix Klein, Hermann

Weyl and others. Hermann Weyl, for example, wrote in 1949 in his "Philosophy of Mathematics and Science" that "Principia" based mathematics:

> "not on logic alone, but on a sort of logician's paradise, a universe endowed with an 'ultimate furniture' of rather complex structure ... Would any realistically-minded man dare say he believes in this transcendental world? ... This complex structure taxes the strength of our faith hardly less than the doctrines of the early Fathers of the Church or of the Scholastic philosophers of the Middle Ages".

The view of this latter group of mathematicians is, broadly speaking, that 'logic rests upon mathematics, and not mathematics upon logic.' Logic according to them is far less reliable than our intuitive concepts, and the development of new mathematics does not require the guarantees of logic. Historically, in any case, logic was abstracted from our experience with already existing mathematical concepts and arguments. Poincaré, for example, once wrote: "Would it be believable that the logicians always proceeded from the general to the particular, as the rules of formal logic seemed to prescribe? By this way they would never have been able to extend the frontiers of science; scientific conquests are only made by generalization."

At another time he wrote:

> "... real mathematics, that which is good for something, may continue to develop in accor-

dance with its own principles without bothering
about the storms of rage outside it, and go on
step by step with its usual conquests which are
final and which it never has to abandon."

Furthermore, the reduction of mathematics to logic could
not succeed in solving all the paradoxes which
threatened the very foundations of mathematics. Even
today, there is still great uncertainty about the precise nature of the foundations of mathematics, while the
role and place of logic is a prominent bone of conten-
tion. Whether a solution will ever be found, is doubtful. In fact, most practising mathematicians today are
disinclined to concern themselves with the precise relationship between mathematics and logic, concentrating
rather on their specialized fields. One thing, however,
mathematicians are agreed upon; logic has a useful role
to play in mathematics. It helps us to achieve a broader
perspective on the logical processes which we use when
we, for instance, construct a proof for a theorem, define a new concept or solve equations.

The purpose of this book is therefore not to get involved in the controversy with regard to the foundations
of mathematics, but to familiarize the reader with an
interesting field in its own right. At the same time it
is hoped that a logical perspective on mathematics will
enable the reader to develop a deeper insight and mas-
tery of mathematics. In everyday life, with all its confusion and uncertainty, it may also be helpful to the
reader to distinguish the logical from the illogical,
and to evaluate the validity of arguments.

This book was stimulated by an in-service course on Logic which the author conducted in July 1986 in Natal. Of course, in Natal a supplementary mathematics curriculum on topics like Integration, Matrices, Numerical Methods, Boolean Algebra, Logic, etc. has been implemented for enrichment to above average pupils for some time. It is hoped that other education departments in South Africa will soon follow Natal's excellent example.

This book is suitable for pupils from Std. 7 - Std. 10, and examples which cover the whole mathematics syllabus in these standards, are given throughout. Since this book was written as a follow-on to "Boolean Algebra at School", and while the same algebraic notation is used, it is recommended that "Boolean Algebra at School" should perhaps be read first. This is, however, not essential since "Elementary Logic" may also be read completely independently (except for one or two examples for which an explicit knowledge of Boolean - or Set Theoretic identities are required).

M.D. de Villiers
Stellenbosch, April 1987

# LOGIC

## 1.    An introductory problem

Mr A and Mr B both collect old manuscripts. Mr A is a collector of English political works and of fictional novels in foreign languages. Mr B is a collector of those non-fictional items that are either works in English or political works in English or political works in foreign languages. Determine which books are collected by both.

## 2.    Discussion

To solve a problem like this it will be necessary for us to examine the exact relationship between Boolean Algebra (see De Villiers (1985)) and Logic. Logic is often defined as the science concerned with the principles of reasoning. In this section we are going to analyze the processes of logical thinking in order to enable us to reduce reasoning to an algebra with fixed and easily applied rules, so that we can easily solve problems like the one above.

Logic is frequently evidenced in daily conversations, e.g.:

"Will you have white coffee or will you have black?"

"I'd rather not have black, if you don't mind."

"Not a bit, the milk is ready."

To make the main argument in the above reasoning clearer, it can be restated as follows:

> Either x or y
> Not y
> So x

Looking at the framework of reasoning as used in the above conversation, it should become clear that in general the soundness of a conclusion does not depend upon the meaning of each word or sentence, but upon correctly drawing a conclusion from the given premises. Of course, in every day life, one frequently finds examples where one may spend a long time arguing about the truth of the premises. In this study of logic we are, however, going to concern ourselves with the making of valid conclusions from any given premises.

## 3.    Propositions and Connectives

A **proposition** may be defined as a statement which is either **true** or **false**, and which cannot be both.

The following may be considered as propositions:

"All men are mortal"

"5 - 3 = 1"

"Western Province won the Currie Cup in 1985."

But the following sentences may not, because some may simply be a matter of opinion, while others cannot be said to be either true or false:

"It is hot today."

"Will you visit us over the week-end?"

"Great shot!"

"Come here."

"Western Province will again win the Currie Cup this year."

The **negation** (or contradiction) of a proposition p is simply another proposition which is true when p is false, and false when p is true. It is written as $\bar{p}$ (read "not p").

**Logical connectives** are used to join propositions. The main ones are:

... and ...   ... or ...   if ... then ...   ... if and only if ...

For example:

p and q ... The orchestra played and the curtain went up.

p or q ... We could eat at Benny's or at Danny's

if p then q ... If you are going shopping then you will need some money.

p if and only if q ... A number is rational if and only if its decimal form terminates or recurs.

## 4.     Conjunction (and: ⋅)

Let us consider the following two statements:

p : x is odd

q : x is prime

and their **conjunction** (p ⋅ q) by the logical connective "and":

r = p.q: x is odd **and** x is prime.

What are the respective truth values of r, p and q in each of the following cases:

1. When x = 6?

2. When x = 2?

3. When x = 9?

4. When x = 3?


Now complete the truth table below if we agree to use the symbol 0 to represent a false proposition and the symbol 1 to represent a true proposition.

$p \qquad q \qquad r = p \cdot q$

| p | q | |
|---|---|---|
| 0 | 0 | |
| 0 | 1 | |
| 1 | 0 | |
| 1 | 1 | |

As a grammatical conjunction in everyday language, how-ever, the word "and" sometimes conveys more than is in-dicated in the above definition. For example, it some-times suggests a **causal** connection as in "He pruned the roses and it never grew again." Sometimes the order of the two clauses makes a difference to the meaning of the words; "He fell upon the dragon and he slew it" is quite different from "He slew the dragon and he fell upon it." In set theory, it should therefore be clear that the propositional connective "and" agrees with the **intersection** of sets, e.g.:

(odd numbers) p          q (prime numbers)

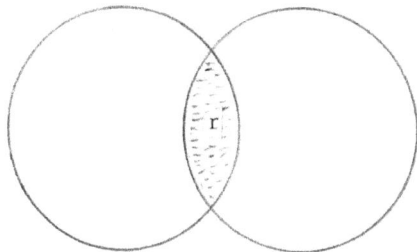

# 5. Disjunction (or : +)

Let us consider the following two statements:

p : x is divisible by 2

q : x is divisible by 3

and their **disjunction** (alternation) by the logical connective "or"

$$r = p + q : x \text{ is divisible by 2 or 3.}$$

Complete the truth table below by considering the following instances:

| | p | q | r = p + q |
|---|---|---|---|
| 1. x = 31 | 0 | 0 | |
| 2. x = 15 | 0 | 1 | |
| 3. x = 14 | 1 | 0 | |
| 4. x = 12 | 1 | 1 | |

When used as a grammatical conjunction in everyday language, the word "or" has two meanings:

**Exclusive** (either one **or** the other **but not both**)

"We must escape now **or** remain prisoners forever"

**Inclusive** (either one **or** the other **or** both – also referred to as and/or).

"Applicants should have mastered in Applied Mathematics or Physics" (A person with both would therefore be acceptable).

Looking at the example above, it should be clear that in logic we have defined the propositional connective "or" with an **inclusive** meaning. This connective in Set Theory agrees with the **union** of sets, e.g.:

(numbers divisible by 2)    q (numbers
                                divisible by 3)
      p

By now you will have noticed the relationship between the logical connectives "or" and "and" and the binary operations of Boolean Algebra. Other logical connectives which are often used in everyday language, are: "neither ... nor ..."; "not both ... and ..." The first logical connective should not be confused with "either ... or ...", which is the same as the disjunctive connective "or". The statement "neither p nor q" can be symbolised by $\overline{(p + q)}$ or, using De Morgan, by $\bar{p}.\bar{q}$. Similarly, the statement "not both p and q" can be symbolized by $\overline{(p.q)}$ or, using De Morgan, by $\bar{p} + \bar{q}$. Using Boolean notation, the earlier introductory problem can now be solved as follows.

7

# 6.    Solution of Introductory Problem

Define: A as the set of books collected by A

B as the set of books collected by B

E as the set of English books

N as the set of fictional novels

P as the set of political works

The books collected by both can be symbolized by
$Z = A \cap B$ or $Z = A \cdot B$ in familiar Boolean notation. Now

1. $A = EP + \bar{E}N$

2. $B = (E + P\bar{E})\bar{N}$

Thus: $Z = (EP + \bar{E}N) \cdot (E + P\bar{E})\bar{N}$ which simplifies to $Z = EP\bar{N}$
by using the various identities of Boolean Algebra. (See
De Villiers (1985) for a listing of these identities).

The non-fictional English political works are therefore
the books collected by both.


# 7.    Exercise

1.    Let  p:  Naas  Botha  was  the  captain  of  the
      Springboks in 1986

      Let q: Durban is the capital of Natal

Let r: The square of a negative number is negative

Say in each case whether the conjunction is true or false.

a) p·q                 b) $\bar{p}$ + q
c) p·$\bar{q}$             d) p·($\bar{q}$·$\bar{r}$)
e) $\bar{q}$·$\bar{r}$            f) ($\bar{p}$ + q) + (p·$\bar{q}$)
g) p + q             h) $\overline{(\bar{p} + q)}$
i) p + $\bar{q}$

2.       Complete the following truth tables

| p | q | $\bar{p}$ | $\bar{q}$ | $\bar{p}·\bar{q}$ | p + q | p + $\bar{p}·q$ | $\overline{p + q}$ |
|---|---|---|---|---|---|---|---|
| 0 | 0 | | | | | | |
| 0 | 1 | | | | | | |
| 1 | 0 | | | | | | |
| 1 | 1 | | | | | | |

Compare the columns with each other. What conclusion(s) can you draw from this?

3.       Let e be the proposition "She is good at English" and m the proposition "She is good at Maths". Express the following compounds in symbols:

       a)      She is good at English and she is good at Maths.

       b)      She is not both good at English and good at Maths.

9

c) She is neither good at English nor good at Maths.

d) It isn't true that she is good at English and not good at Maths.

(e) She is either good at English or at Maths.

4. Which of the following are propositions?

(a) I have eaten a cake in the last ten minutes.

(b) Are you feeling well?

(c) Ann said, "Are you feeling well?"

(d) Sit down!

(e) This sentence is not a proposition.

5. If p represents: "Blondes are beautiful"

If q represents "Brunettes are fickle"

If r represents "School-boys are perplexed by logic"

write out the full meaning of the following in reasonable English:

(a) $p.q$     (b) $p + \bar{q}$     (c) $\bar{p}.q$
(d) $p.q + r$     (e) $\bar{p}.q + p.\bar{q}$     (f) $p.\bar{q}.\bar{r}$

6. If a represents "John wants to go to the dance" and b represents "John wants to read a book" then symbolize the following compound propositions:

(a) John does not want to go to the dance tonight.

10

(b)     John either wants to go to the dance or to read a book, or possibly both.

(c)     John does not want to go to the dance nor to read a book.

(d)     John does not want to go to the dance but wants to read a book.

(e)     Either John wants to read a book and not go to the dance, or he wants to go to the dance and not read a book.

7.     Which of the following pairs convey the same information? (Check that they have the same truth tables)

a) 1.   It is not true that he is a philosopher and a man of action.

   2.   He is not a philosopher and he is not a man of action.

b) 1.   Either he is not a coward or he is not telling the truth.

   2.   It is not true that he is a coward and that he is truthful.

8.     Honest Harvey, a second-hand car dealer, has a number of cream-coloured eight cylinder cars. He also has cars with airconditioning and with less than eight cylinders. Another dealer, Mad Dan, has cars without airconditioning and eight cylinders. He also has eight cylinder models with airconditioning and a couple of cream-coloured cars.

Find:

a)   those categories of cars sold by both dealers

b)   all the different categories of cars marketed by the two dealers collectively

c)   those categories of cars which are not sold by Honest Harvey

d)   those categories of cars which are not sold by Mad Dan.

9.   Three friends are all keen collectors of bus tickets. Tom collects the tickets of country double-decker buses, all double-decker buses and town single-decker buses. Dick prefers to collect the tickets of town double-decker buses and also collects all country buses. Harry collects town buses, single-decker buses and single-decker country buses. Write down expressions for the vehicle tickets collected by each of the friends. What types do both Tom and Dick collect? Are there any types which Tom and Dick collect but which Harry does not collect?

# 8.   Equivalence/biconditional (if and only if: $\Longleftrightarrow$ )

Let us consider the following two statements:

p : x is even
q : x is divisible by 2
and the biconditional
p $\Longleftrightarrow$ q:   x is even if and only if it is divisible by 2.

From the above it should be clear that a biconditional is true whenever p and q have the same truth value. It is defined by the truth table:

p    q    p⟺q

| p | q | p⟺q |
|---|---|---|
| 0 | 0 | 1 |
| 0 | 1 | 0 |
| 1 | 0 | 0 |
| 1 | 1 | 1 |

## 9. Implication/conditional (if ... then: ⟹ )

"Pure mathematics is the class of all propositions of the form 'p implies q', where p and q are propositions containing one or more variables, the same in the two propositions, and neither p nor q contains any constants except logical constants." - Bertrand Russell

The implication connective is used in everyday language in a great many ways.

1.    If you come any nearer, then I shall fire.

2.    If they had trained harder, then they might have won.

3.    If he were under oath, then I might believe him.

4.    If triangle ABC is isosceles, then two sides must be equal.

5.    If current passes through the wire, then it will glow.

These examples suggest intention, conjecture over the past, doubt, analysis and cause.

The implication (p $\Rightarrow$ q) is defined by the following table:

| p | q | p $\Rightarrow$ q |
|---|---|---|
| 0 | 0 | 1 |
| 0 | 1 | 1 |
| 1 | 0 | 0 |
| 1 | 1 | 1 |

In the implication (p $\Rightarrow$ q), p is called the **hypothesis** (antecedent or premise) and q is called the **conclusion** (consequent).

Many people may have difficulty accepting the truth of a conditional with a false hypothesis since this convention may not correspond with common usage as he perceives it. To show that the truth table for p    q agrees to a certain degree with "common sense", let us analyze an example in which a father promises his son, "If your attendance record at school this term is good, then I'll give you a bicycle." At the end of the term, the son will pronounce judgement on the truth of his father's conditional statement according to which of the four following possibilities occurs.

1.      The boy actually does have a good attendance record, and his father does give him a bicycle. The boy will feel his father was telling the truth. Here we have the last row of the truth

14

table, namely truth values 1, 1, 1 for p, q, p $\Rightarrow$ q respectively.

2.      The boy's attendance is good, but his father does not present him with a bicycle. "Dad, you were not telling the truth", the youngster says. Here we have the third row of the truth table.

3.      The boy's attendance is not good, but nevertheless his father does give him a bicycle. Since the father made no threat, that is did not cover the contingency just described, the boy would not question the truth of the original statement, and hence we have the second row of the truth table.

4.      The boy's attendance is not good and his father does not give him a bicycle. The boy will feel that his father's behaviour is just, and hence will not accuse his parent of making a false promise. This gives us the first row of the truth table.

Some people may feel that they do not have sufficient information to decide whether a statement is true or false when the hypothesis is false. For instance, when the boy's attendance is not good, one may feel that one cannot say whether the original statement is true or false. However, since such ambiguities are unacceptable in a mathematical system, it is agreed among mathematicians to assign the truth value "true" in all those cases where the hypothesis is false.

15

For practice in the meaning of this definition of implication, the reader should convince himself that the statement "If 1 + 1 = 2, then Kimberley is the capital of the Orange Free State" is false whereas the following "If 1 + 1 = 5, then Kimberley is the capital of the Orange Free State" is true. What is therefore assumed in the truth table, is that p $\Rightarrow$ q is false only when the hypothesis is true and the conclusion is false.

In mathematics, of course, we are not really interested in false hypotheses. When we attempt to prove the validity of an implication p => q in mathematics, we assume that p is true. Our goal is then to reach the conclusion that q is also true. To disprove an implication in mathematics, it is sufficient to show that q is false despite the assumed validity of p. In mathematics we are therefore mostly interested only in the last two rows of the earlier truth table definition of an implication.

Another formulation the implication p $\Rightarrow$ q may take is "p only if q". If one does not readily see the equivalence of "if p then q" and "p only if q", the following example may help:

"If a person lives in Pietermaritzburg, then he lives in Natal."

"A person lives in Pietermaritzburg, only if he also lives in Natal." (E.g. he cannot be living in Pietermaritzburg while at the same time not living in Natal!)

16

# 10.    Converse, inverse and contrapositive

> "... it is not true to say that where there's
> number there's the odd, whereas it is true to
> say that where there's the odd, there's
> number." - Socrates in Plato's "The Trial and
> Death of Socrates"

Closely connected to an implication are its converse,
inverse and contrapositive:

$p \Rightarrow q$ implication

$q \Rightarrow p$ converse

$\bar{p} \Rightarrow \bar{q}$ inverse

$\bar{q} \Rightarrow \bar{p}$ contrapositive

Complete the following truth tables:

| p | q | $p \Rightarrow q$ | $q \Rightarrow p$ | $\bar{p} \Rightarrow \bar{q}$ | $\bar{q} \Rightarrow \bar{p}$ |
|---|---|---|---|---|---|
| 0 | 0 | | | | |
| 0 | 1 | | | | |
| 1 | 0 | | | | |
| 1 | 1 | | | | |
| | | Implica-tion | Converse | Inverse | Contraposi-tive |

From these truth tables, it can be seen that an
implication and its contrapositive are equivalent, but
that an implication is not (in general) equivalent to
its converse or inverse.

17

"If ABCD is a square, then ABCD has four sides" is equivalent to:

"If ABCD does not have four sides, then ABCD is not a square", but it is not equivalent to:

"If ABCD has four sides, then ABCD is a square" or to:

"If ABCD is not a square, then ABCD does not have four sides."

Of course, there are also many examples of true statements like "If a woman lives in Cape Town, then she lives in the capital of the Cape Province" which do have true converses and inverses. But in general, this is not always the case! The implication p $\Rightarrow$ q is also often translated in the form

1.    p implies q

2.    p is sufficient for q

3.    q is necessary for p

A simple example from Euclidean geometry illustrates the important meanings of the last two forms:

Suppose p = (the triangles ABC and DEF are congruent)

q = (the triangles ABC and DEF are equal in area)

18

Then in Euclidean geometry  p $\Rightarrow$ q

We may translate this remark as:

p is a **sufficient** condition for q.

If we are trying to show that the triangles are equal in area, and we manage to show that they are congruent, then that is sufficient: there is no more to be done. This type of phrase is very common in mathematics and is not to be confused with the similar phrase:

q is a **necessary** condition for p.

This second phrase means exactly the same as the first. It is another translation of p $\Rightarrow$ q. You will see that the triangles must be equal in area in order that they be congruent: however, equality of area is not in itself enough to ensure congruence. q is <u>not</u> a sufficient condition for p. Nor do two triangles have to be congruent in order to be equal in area. p is <u>not</u> a necessary condition for q. This distinction between necessary and sufficient conditions is an important one, and must always be borne in mind.

Since p => q is equivalent to saying that q is a necessary condition for p, an implication is sometimes also formulated as follows:

"Only if q, then p."

For instance, saying "If a quadrilateral is a square, then it is a rectangle" is the same as saying "Only if a quadrilateral is a rectangle, can it be a square."

Now it may happen that a condition is both necessary and sufficient. For instance, let

p = this triangle has two equal sides

q = this triangle has two equal angles

For a triangle to be isosceles (p), it is necessary that two angles should be equal (q), and this condition is also sufficient. Once we have shown that two angles are equal, there is no more te be done. What we therefore have is an equivalence connective:

"a triangle is isosceles if and only if two angles are equal"

or in symbols:  $p \Longleftrightarrow q$

(Of course, another way of translating the above is to say p implies and is implied by q. It therefore also means that both the implication and its converse are true).

Some other examples:

a)     $x = 2$ is a sufficient condition that $x^2 = 4$

       $(x = 2 \Rightarrow x^2 = 4)$

       but it is not a necessary condition.

b)     xy is odd is a sufficient and necessary condition
       that x is odd and y odd.

       (xy is odd $\Leftrightarrow$ x is odd and y is odd)

# 11.  Illogical Propositional Reasoning

It often happens that people draw illogical conclusions
even from a statement that we accept to be true. One of
the ways in which this frequently occurs, is by confusing a statement and its converse or by confusing it
with its inverse.

The statement

      "If he is in trouble with the law, then the po-
      lice come for him"

has as converse

      "If the police come for him, then he is in
      trouble with the law"

21

Even if the first statement is accepted as true, it is quite illogical for inquisitive neighbours to assume the truth of the second statement. Similarly, many people starting from the (doubtful) statement

"If it is an expensive product, you can rely on its quality" illogically conclude that the inverse is also true:

"If it is not an expensive product, you cannot rely on its quality"

Of course, we may use the fact that an implication and its contrapositive are equivalent. For instance, the statement:

"If the velocity of light as observed by us depends on the velocity of the earth through the ether, then light reflected from equal distances in different directions will return to us at different times"

led to the famous Michelson-Morley experiment at the end of the last century which surprisingly gave the negation of the second part of this proposition - in fact, the different rays of light returned at the same time. This in turn implied the negation of the first part - the velocity of light as observed by us does not depend on the velocity of the earth through space: and this is one of the foundations of the special theory of relativity.

## 12.    Exercise

1.    p = (tomorrow will be a fine day)

q = (we shall take a trip to the coast)

Write down the meaning of the following propositions in reasonable English:

(a) $p \Rightarrow q$   (b) $q \Rightarrow p$   (c) $\bar{p} \Rightarrow \bar{q}$   (d) $\bar{q} \Rightarrow \bar{p}$

Assuming the truth of (a), which of the others are true?

2.    p = (this quadrilateral is a rhombus)

q = (this quadrilateral has perpendicular
diagonals)

Write down the meaning of the following propositions in
reasonable English:

(a) $p \Rightarrow q$   (b) $q \Rightarrow p$   (c) $\bar{p} \Rightarrow \bar{q}$   (d) $\bar{q} \Rightarrow \bar{p}$

Assuming the truth of (a), which of the others
are true?

3.    Let p be the statement, "I go to bed early", and
q be the statement, "I feel very well". Express
the following in symbols:

(a)    I go to bed early and feel very well

(b)    If I go to bed early, then I feel very
well

(c)    I go to bed early only if I do not feel
very well

23

(c)      I go to bed early only if I do not feel very well

(d)      I feel very well if I do not go to bed early.

4.      Complete the truth tables of the following:

| p | q | $\bar{p}$ | $\bar{q}$ | $p \Rightarrow q$ | $\overline{(p \Rightarrow q)}$ | $\bar{p} \Rightarrow q$ | $\bar{p} \Leftrightarrow q$ |
|---|---|---|---|---|---|---|---|
| 0 | 0 | | | | | | |
| 0 | 1 | | | | | | |
| 1 | 0 | | | | | | |
| 1 | 1 | | | | | | |

5.      Establish that the following propositions are equivalent. (Check their truth tables).

$$p \Rightarrow q \quad \text{and} \quad \bar{p} + q \quad \text{and} \quad \overline{(p \cdot \bar{q})}$$

6.      State the contrapositives of the following:

(a)      If he is good, he need not feel afraid

(b)      If x is even, then xy will be even

(c)      If triangles are congruent, then they are similar

7.      Establish that the following propositions are equivalent. (Check their truth tables)

$$p \Leftrightarrow q \quad \text{and} \quad (p \Rightarrow q) \cdot (q \Rightarrow p)$$

Translate the last proposition into English.

8. Consider the following scene at home.

   (a) Your mother says: "If you have finished your homework, then you may watch television."

   Are you **logically** obliged to finish your homework before you watch television? (The author does not take any responsibility if your mother doesn't believe you!)

   (b) What if your mother had instead said:

   "If you have not finished your homework, then you may not watch television"? Would you then logically be obliged to comply to her wishes?

   (c) Formulate the converse of your mother's statement in (a). (Hint: use the form: p only if q).

   Would you be logically obliged to comply to her wishes if she had said the converse instead of the original statement?

9. State for each of the following conditions whether it is

   (i) necessary and sufficient or

   (ii) necessary but not sufficient or

   (iii) not necessary but sufficient or

   (iv) neither necessary nor sufficient

   (a) A _____ condition that a number is divisible by two is that its last digit is even.

   (b) A _____ condition that a number is divisible by 3 is that the last digit is 3.

25

(c)     A _____ condition that a number is divisible by 4 is that the number formed by the last two digits is divisible by 10.

(d)     A _____ condition that a number is divisible by 5 is that its last digit is zero.

(e)     A _____ condition that a number is divisible by 6 is that it is divisible by 2 or it is divisible by 3.

(f)     A _____ condition that a number is divisible by 10 is that its last two digits are zero.

(g)     A _____ condition that a kite is a rhombus is that it has one pair of opposite sides parallel.

(h)     A _____ condition that a cyclic quadrilateral has at least one pair of opposite sides parallel, is that at least three of its sides must be equal.

(i)     A _____ condition that a quadrilateral is cyclic is that it has at least one opposite pair of right angles.

(j)     A _____ condition that a kite is cyclic is that it has at least one opposite pair of right angles.

(k)     A _____ condition that two triangles are congruent is that they correspondingly have a non-enclosed angle and two sides equal provided the side opposite the angle is greater than the other side.

(l)     A _____ condition that $y = mx + c$ is a tangent to $y = ax^2 + bx + c$ is that the discriminant $\Delta = 0$ for $mx + x = ax^2 + bx + c$.

(m)    A _____ condition that f(x) has a local minimum at x=a is that the second derivative is equal to zero for x=a; or in other words, f" (a) = 0.

10.    State whether the following are necessary, sufficient, or necessary and sufficient.

(a)    2 angles are equal is a _____ condition for a triangle to be equilateral.

(b)    The diagonals cross at right angles is a _____ condition for a quadrilateral to be a square.

(c)    The diagonals bisect each other is a _____ condition for a quadrilateral to be a parallelogram.

(d)    The 4 sides are equal is a _____ condition for a quadrilateral to be a rhombus.

(e)    One pair of opposite angles are equal is a _____ condition for a quadrilateral to be a kite.

(f)    Two sides and any angle of a triangle correspondingly equal to those of another triangle, is a _____ condition for them to be congruent.

(g)    Two angles of a triangle correspondingly equal to two angles of another triangle is a _____ condition for them to be similar.

(h)    Three angles of a quadrilateral correspondingly equal to three angles of another quadrilateral, is a _____ condition for them to be similar.

(i)  For a quadratic equation to have rational roots it is a _____ condition that the discriminant either be a complete square or zero.

(j)  The discriminant is a complete square or zero, is a _____ condition for a quadratic equation to have real roots.

(k)  $f(x) = f(-x)$ for all x is a _____ condition for a function $f(x)$ to be symmetrical around the y-axis.

(l)  $f'(a)=0$ is a _____ condition for the graph of the function $f(x)$ to have a point of inflexion at x=a.

(m)  The function $f(x)$ has a local maximum point at x=a is a _____ condition for $f'(a)=0$.

(n)  The product of the gradients $m_1$, and $m_2$ of two straight lines is -1, is a _____ condition for the two lines to be perpendicular.

(o)  Equal corresponding angles formed by an intersecting transversal of two lines, is a _____ condition for the two lines to be parallel.

(p)  sin x=sin y is a _____ condition for x=y.

11.  In the algebra of real numbers, which of the following are true:

(a) $x^2 = 4 \Rightarrow x = 2$

(b) $2x > 8 \Leftrightarrow x > 4$

(c) $(x - 1)(x - 3) < 0 \Rightarrow 1 < x < 3$

(d) $\frac{1}{x} = 0 \Rightarrow x = 0$

(e) $x = 3 \Rightarrow x^2 = 9$

(f) $x^2 = 9 \Leftrightarrow x = 3$ or $x = -3$

12.    Connect each of the following statements in the algebra of real numbers with the appropriate symbol, $\Rightarrow$ , $\Leftrightarrow$ , or $\not\Rightarrow$ .

(a) $x = 0$               $xy = 0$

(b) $xy = 0$          $x = 0$, or $y = 0$, or both

(c) $x^{\frac{1}{2}} = 4$          $x = 16$

(d) $-3x + 12 \geq 0$     $x \leq 4$

(e) $x^2 + x - 2 = 0$     $x = 1$

(f) $\sin x = \frac{1}{2}$         $x = 60^\circ$

(g) $|x| = 2$          $x = 2$

(h) $\log (x-1) + \log (x-4) = 1$    $x = -1$ or $x = 6$

(i) $x = 0, \overset{\bullet}{9}$         $x = 1$

13.

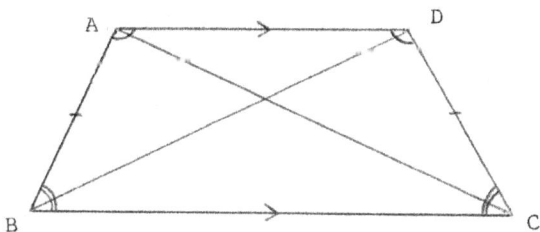

The above figure is called an isosceles trapezium. It has the following properties:

(1)  AD//BC    (2)  AB=DC    (3)  AC=DB
(4)  $\hat{A}=\hat{D}$       (5)  $\hat{B}=\hat{C}$      (6)  $\hat{A}+\hat{C} = 180^\circ = \hat{B}+\hat{D}$

In defining mathematical concepts we usually only pick those properties that are necessary and sufficient conditions. Which of the following are both necessary and sufficient conditions for a quadrilateral to be an isosceles trapezium? (If they are necessary and sufficient, show that the other properties may be deduced from them).

(a)　An isosceles trapezium is any quadrilateral with two pairs of adjacent angles equal.

(b)　An isosceles trapezium is a cyclic quadrilateral with at least one pair of opposite sides equal.

(c)　An isosceles trapezium is any quadrilateral with at least one pair of opposite sides parallel.

(d)　An isosceles trapezium is any quadrilateral with equal diagonals.

(e)　An isosceles trapezium is a cyclic quadrilateral with equal diagonals.

(f)　An isosceles trapezium is a trapezium with both pairs of opposite angles supplementary.

Which of the above would you personally prefer as a definition? Why?

14.

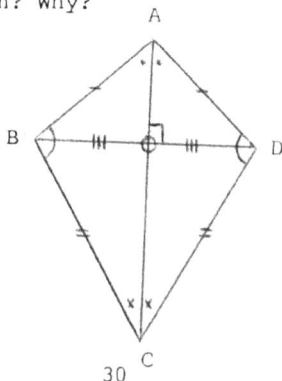

The above figure is called a kite. It has the
following properties:

(1)  AB = AD                    (5)  $B\hat{A}O = D\hat{A}O$
(2)  CB = CD                    (6)  $B\hat{C}O = D\hat{C}O$
(3)  BO = OD                    (7)  $A\hat{B}C = A\hat{D}C$
(4)  AC $\perp$ BD


Which of the following are necessary and sufficient conditions for a quadrilateral to be a
kite? Check your conclusions by confirming if the
other properties may be deduced from the definitions below.

(a)   A kite is any quadrilateral with perpen-
      dicular diagonals.

(b)   Any quadrilateral ABCD is a kite, if the
      diagonals are perpendicular and the one
      diagonal bisects the other.

(c)   A kite is any quadrilateral with two
      pairs of adjacent sides equal, as well as
      perpendicular diagonals.

(d)   A kite is any quadrilateral with at least
      one pair of opposite angles equal.

(e)   A kite is any quadrilateral with at least
      one pair of opposite angles equal, as
      well as perpendicular diagonals.

(f)   A kite is any quadrilateral with the one
      diagonal bisecting a pair of opposite an-
      gles as well as the other diagonal.

Rectify the **incomplete** definitions above (those
that have necessary but not sufficient conditions) by including more properties. Also make
the **uneconomical** definitions above (those that
have sufficient, but more than necessary condi-

31

tions) economical, by deleting redundant properties which may be deduced from others already
given in the definition. (Note: Compare the cri-
teria for mathematical definitions with those for
the choice of axioms for a mathematical system
(See De Villiers, 1985)).

15.  For a quadrilateral to be a cyclic quadrilateral,
     it is a necessary and sufficient condition that
     the sums of the pairs of opposite angles are
     equal. Find a necessary and sufficient condition
     for a quadrilateral to be a circum-quadrilateral,
     that is a quadrilateral circumscribed around a
     circle as shown below. Now compare the conditions
     for a cyclic quadrilateral and a circum-quadri-
     lateral. What do you notice?

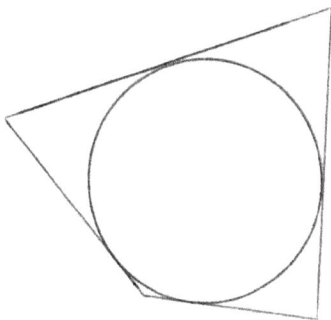

16.  Consider the following implication:

     "The sum of two even integers is odd."

     Do the folowing examples **disprove** the implica-
     tion?

(a)    3 + 5 = 8

(b)    3 + 4 = 7

Explain your answer.

# 13.    Validating Arguments and Solving Problems

One of the main reasons for studying Logic is to find out if arguments like the following are valid or invalid:

> "If there is a storm then there is interference on the television. There is a storm. There will be interference."

or solve a "mystery" problem like:

> "Either Fred or Sam murdered Mr Green. If Sam murdered Mr Green, then the butler was off Thursday night. If the butler was off Thursday night, then Nurse Partridge did not witness the crime. However, it is known that nurse Partridge did witness the crime. Who murdered Mr Green?"

In order to do this, however, we will first have to bring in some more terminology, which will be introduced in the following paragraphs.

# 14. Tautology

Consider the compound proposition:

"I am, or am not, wearing black shoes today".

It tells us nothing new for it is always true whether or not I actually am wearing black shoes. We can see this more easily if we draw the truth table.

Let p be the proposition "I am wearing black shoes today". Then my original compound statement, which could be restated as, "Either I am wearing black shoes today, or I am not wearing black shoes today", can be put symbolically as $p + \bar{p}$

The truth table is:

| p | $\bar{p}$ | $p + \bar{p}$ |
|---|-----------|---------------|
| 0 | 1 | 1 |
| 1 | 0 | 1 |

and it can be seen that $p + \bar{p}$ is **always true**. Any proposition like this, which is always true (regardless of the truth of its elements) is called a **tautology**. (This particular tautology namely, $p + \bar{p}$, is also known as the Law of the Excluded Middle).

## 15.    Contradiction

Consider the compound proposition

> "I both am, and am not, wearing a green tie to-
> day".

If p is the proposition, "I am wearing a green tie today" then my original statement, put in the form

> "I am wearing a green tie today, and I am not
> wearing a green tie today"

is symbolically  p . $\bar{p}$

It is clearly never true in any circumstance, and can
easily be verified by completing its truth table. Any
such proposition which is **always false** is known as a
**contradiction**.

## 16.    Logically Indeterminate

Of course, in many cases propositions are neither tautologies nor contradictions. For instance, the implication connective we had earlier is neither always true
nor always false. If a proposition is sometimes true and
sometimes false, it is called **logically indeterminate**,
since its value depends on the actual truth of the pre-
misse.

# 17.    Logical Equivalence

Earlier on in the section on Boolean Algebra (see De
Villiers (1985)), we defined the logical equivalence between two propositions by saying that for the same input
values they must always give the same output values. For
instance, to prove that the expressions $p * (q + r)$ and
$(p \cdot q) + (p * r)$ were logically equivalent, we set up
truth tables and checked whether they gave the same output values for the same input values, e.g.

| p | q | r | $p * (q + r)$ | $(p \cdot q) + (p * r)$ |
|---|---|---|---|---|
| 0 | 0 | 0 | 0 | 0 |
| 0 | 0 | 1 | 0 | 0 |
| 0 | 1 | 0 | 0 | 0 |
| 0 | 1 | 1 | 0 | 0 |
| 1 | 0 | 0 | 0 | 0 |
| 1 | 0 | 1 | 1 | 1 |
| 1 | 1 | 0 | 1 | 1 |
| 1 | 1 | 1 | 1 | 1 |

Looking at it from the concepts of Logic just introduced, it is the same as asking to prove that

$$p \cdot (q + r) \Leftrightarrow (p \cdot q) + (p \cdot r)$$

is **always true**, and therefore a **tautology**. This can
easily be done, by applying the definition of the equivalence implication (namely that a b is true whenever a
and b have the same values) to the last two columns
above. Thus,

| p | q | r | p·(q+r) | (p,q)+ (p·r) | p·(q+r)⟺(p,q)+(p·r) |
|---|---|---|---------|--------------|-------------------------|
| 0 | 0 | 0 | 0 | 0 | 1 |
| 0 | 0 | 1 | 0 | 0 | 1 |
| 0 | 1 | 0 | 0 | 0 | 1 |
| 0 | 1 | 1 | 0 | 0 | 1 |
| 1 | 0 | 0 | 0 | 0 | 1 |
| 1 | 0 | 1 | 1 | 1 | 1 |
| 1 | 1 | 0 | 1 | 1 | 1 |
| 1 | 1 | 1 | 1 | 1 | 1 |

From this, we can see that our earlier collection of Boolean statements, since consisting of equivalent expressions, are all tautologies.

## 18.　Exercise

1.　Which of the following are tautologies, contradictions or logically indeterminate? (Construct their truth tables, if necessary).

(a) $p \Rightarrow p$　　　　　　　　(b) $p \cdot \overline{(p + q)}$

(c) $p \Rightarrow (p + q)$　　　　　(d) $\overline{(p + q)} \cdot p$

(e) $(p \Rightarrow q) + q$　　　　　(f) $\overline{(p + q)} \Longleftrightarrow \bar{p} \cdot \bar{q}$

(g) $p \cdot (q \cdot \bar{q})$　　　　　　(h) $pq \Rightarrow p$

(i) $p + q \Longleftrightarrow q + p$　　　(j) $\bar{p} \Rightarrow (p \Rightarrow q)$

(k) $q \Rightarrow p \cdot \bar{p}$　　　　　(l) $p + (q + \bar{q}) \Longleftrightarrow p$

(m) $\overline{(p + q)} \Rightarrow \bar{p}$　　　(n) $(p + q) \cdot \bar{p}$

(o) $[(p \Rightarrow q) \cdot p] \Rightarrow q$　　(p) $[(p+q) \cdot \bar{p}] \Rightarrow q$

2.(i)　By constructing truth tables, determine which of the following are tautologies:

　　(a)　　$p \Rightarrow [(p + q) + r]$　(b) $p \cdot q \Rightarrow \overline{(p + r)}$

　　(c)　　$p \Rightarrow (\bar{p} \Rightarrow q)$

37

(ii)     If p stands for "I am wearing a red tie"

q stands for "I am wearing a white shirt"

r stands for "I am wearing a yellow waistcoat" then translate each of the above compound propositions into reasonable English.

3.       Are the following true? In each case, check your conclusion by expressing the propositions symbolically and seeing from truth tables whether the formulae are logically equivalent.

(a)     "If $x = 60^{\circ}$, then $\cos x = \frac{1}{2}$," is the same thing as "If $\cos x = \frac{1}{2}$, then $x = 60^{\circ}$"

(b)     The two statements: "If the opposite angles of a quadrilateral are supplementary, then it is a cyclic quadrilateral" and "If the quadrilateral is cyclic, then the opposite angles are supplementary" are equivalent to saying "A quadrilateral has supplementary opposite angles if and only if it is cyclic."

(c)     The two statements: "If a transversal intersects two lines and the sum of the interior angles on the same side of the transversal is $180^{\circ}$, then the two lines are parallel", and "If two parallel lines are intersected by a transversal, then the sum of the interior angles on the same side of the transversal is $180^{\circ}$" are equivalent to saying "If a transversal intersects two lines, these two lines are parallel if, and only if, the sum of the interior angles on the same side of the transversal is $180^{\circ}$.

(d)   The two statements: "If $\log_x 8 = 3$, then $x = 2$" and "If $x = 2$, then $\log_x 8 = 3$" are equivalent to saying "$x = 2$, if, and only if, $\log_x 8 = 3$"

(e)   "If $x = -3$, then $|x| = 3$" is the same thing as "If $|x| = 3$, then $x = -3$"

4.   Let a be the proposition $p \Rightarrow q$

Let b be the proposition $q \Rightarrow r$

Let c be the proposition $p \Rightarrow r$

Show that $a \cdot b \Rightarrow c$ is a tautology.

5.   Investigate the validity of the following conjecture and its converse:

"If n is an even integer, then $n^2$ is even."

Try to prove both the conjecture and its converse.

6.   Rewrite each of the following implications in two different equivalent forms.

(a)   If the diagonals of a quadrilateral bisect each other, then the quadrilateral is a parallelogram.

(b)   The sum of two odd integers is even.

(c)   If two angles of a triangle are equal, the sides opposite them are equal.

(d)   The medians of a triangle are concurrent.

(e)   Two numbers m and n are odd only if their product is odd.

(f)     Only if the vector sum of all forces act-
        ing on a body is zero, is the body in
        static equilibrium.

(g)     Only if $x^2 = 16$, is $x = 4$.

7.      Two definitions are logically equivalent if the
        one implies the other, and vice versa. Prove that
        the following pairs of definitions are logically
        equivalent.

        (a)     A parallelogram is a quadrilateral with
                bisecting diagonals.

                A parallelogram is a quadrilateral with
                both pairs of opposite angles equal.

        (b)     A rhombus is a kite with bisecting diago-
                nals.

                A rhombus is a parallelogram with perpen-
                dicular diagonals.

# 19.    Rules of Logic

"We must devise a general technique by which
all reasoning can be reduced to mere calcula-
tion. This method should serve at the same time
as a sort of universal language, whose symbols
and special vocabulary can direct reasoning in
such a way that errors, except those of fact
will be like mistakes in computation, merely a
result of failure to apply the rules correctly." – Gottfried Wilhelm Leibniz


"I will exhibit logic, in its practical aspect,
as a system of processes carried on by the aid
of symbols having a definite interpretation,
and subject to laws founded upon that interpretation alone. But at the same time these laws

are identical in form with the laws of algebra
... "   - George Boole in "Laws of Thought"


By now you have probably realised that in order to determine whether the argument

1.      If there is a storm then there is interference on
        the television.

2.      There is a storm.

3.      There will be interference.


is valid, we only have to translate it into symbols, and
check to see if it forms a tautology. For instance, if p
is the proposition

        "There is a storm"

        and q is the proposition

        "There will be interference on the television"

        then the argument can be put symbolically as

        $[(p \Rightarrow q) \quad .p] \Rightarrow q$


Now complete the truth table below

| p | q | $p \Rightarrow q$ | $(p \Rightarrow q) \cdot p$ | $[(p \Rightarrow q) \cdot p] \Rightarrow q$ |
|---|---|---|---|---|
| 0 | 0 | 1 | 0 | |
| 0 | 1 | 1 | 0 | |
| 1 | 0 | 0 | 0 | |
| 1 | 1 | 1 | 1 | |

Since the final column is always true, we have a tautology and we can say that the argument is valid. This, of course, we expected, because in everyday language we have always intuitively assumed that arguments of this form are sound.

# Rule 1

This specific form of argument so frequently occurs in such a variety of places, for instance,

In law:

$p \Rightarrow q$   If Smith was in Europe at the time a burglary was committed in Cape Town, then he did not commit that crime

$p$   (There is incontestable evidence that) Smith was in Europe at the time.

$\Rightarrow q$   Smith did not commit the crime.

In mathematics:

$p \Rightarrow q$   If this triangle has two equal angles, then it has two equal sides;

$p$   but this triangle has two equal angles

$\Rightarrow q$   Therefore this triangle has two equal sides.

that it is known as the **Law of Detachment** (Modus Ponens). In words, it states that "if both an implication

$p \Rightarrow q$ and its premise p are true, then its consequent q can be **detached** and asserted to be true." It is customary and convenient to also write the law of Detachment as follows:

$$\frac{\begin{array}{c} p \Rightarrow q \\ p \end{array}}{\Rightarrow q}$$

Modus Ponens is the most frequently used rule of Logic in mathematical proof. Consider for instance, the proof of the following well-known implication.

**To prove:**

If a triangle is isosceles, then its base angles are equal.

**Construction:**

Draw AD $\perp$ BC for the given $\triangle$ ABC where AB = AC.

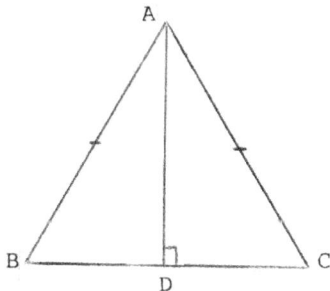

**Proof:**

In $\triangle$ ABD and $\triangle$ ACD:

(1)      AB = AC ... given

(2)      $B\hat{D}A = 90'' = C\hat{D}A$ ... construction

(3)     AD is common

Thus, $\triangle$ ABD $\equiv$ $\triangle$ ACD ... (S, S, $90°$)

$\therefore$ $A\hat{B}D$ = $A\hat{C}D$

**Discussion:**

Let p: AB = AC

Let q: $\begin{cases} p \\ B\hat{D}A = 90° = C\hat{D}A \\ AD = AD \end{cases}$

Ler r: $\triangle$ ABD $\equiv$ $\triangle$ ACD

Let s:    $A\hat{B}D$ = $A\hat{C}D$


The logical structure of the proof clearly consists of two consecutive applications of Modus Ponens, e.g.:

[q . (q => r)] => r

[r . (r => s)] => s


We have therefore shown that if p is given or assumed as **true** (therefore also q); it implies according to Modus Ponens (or alternately syllogism in combination with Modus Ponens) that s will also be **true**. Thus we have proved the validity of the implication p => s. (Note that q => r is accepted as an axiom in our school geometry, but can be proved in more rigorous approaches. The

44

validity of the implication r => s follows directly from the definition of congruence.)

As stated in the very beginning of our discussion of the propositional calculus, a major issue is the search for universal truths or tautologies, that is, logical forms which result in true propositions when any propositions whatsoever are substituted for the variables (p, q, r, etc.) which the form contain. Another way of saying it, is to say that we are looking for **rules of logic** or **rules of inference** such as the (Law of Detachment) above by which we can easily derive the correct conclusions from given premises, or judge the validity or invalidity of given arguments. Since there are obviously very many different tautologies, we are going to confine ourselves to those most frequently used.

# Rule 2

The **law of the Contrapositive** is simply a formalization of our previous work with the contrapositive of an implication. It states that an implication and its contrapositive always have the same value, therefore that $(p \Rightarrow q) \Leftrightarrow (\bar{q} \Rightarrow \bar{p})$ is a tautology. Using this law we may from "If a is less than zero, then $a^2$ is greater than zero" conclude that "If $a^2$ is not greater than zero, then a is not less than zero."

# Rule 3

The **rule of Disjunctive Inference** states that if a disjunction is true, and one of its disjuncts is false, then the other disjunct is true. In symbols:

$$\left[(p + q) \cdot \bar{p}\right] \Rightarrow q \quad \text{and} \quad \left[(p + q) \cdot \bar{q}\right] \Rightarrow p$$

Examples:

1.  From $a = 0$ or $b = 0$, and $a \neq 0$, we may conclude that $b = 0$

2.  From "Mr Clark's arthritis is acting up again or his daughter did not pass Zulu", and "His daughter passed Zulu", we may conclude that "Mr Clark's arthritis is acting up again."

The previous example may be presented in statement-reason form as follows:

Let p represent "Mr Clark's arthritis is acting up again"

Let q represent "Mr Clark's daughter passed Zulu"

| | Statements | Reason |
|---|---|---|
| 1. | $p + \bar{q}$ | Given |
| 2. | $q$ | Given |
| 3. | $p$ | Rule 3 on Steps 1 and 2 |

Another frequently used form of argument, is the following:

"If a man lives in De Aar, then he lives in the Cape Province."

"If he lives in the Cape Province, then he lives in South Africa."

Therefore,

"If he lives in De Aar, then he lives in South Africa."

# Rule 4

This form of argument or rule of inference is known as the **Law of Syllogism** and is in symbols:

$$\left[(p \Rightarrow q) \cdot (q \Rightarrow r)\right] \Rightarrow (p \Rightarrow r)$$

The law of syllogism dates back to the old Greeks who already formalized it. The proof in terms of a truth table was already done as no 4 in the previous exercise. It can also be written as follows

$p \Rightarrow q$

$\dfrac{q \Rightarrow r}{p \Rightarrow r}$

The law of Syllogism also provides an effective illustration of the essential distinction between the validity of a logical process as a whole and the truth of an individual premise involved in the process. Consider, for example, how using <u>valid</u> reasoning, a conclusion is

47

drawn from false premises in the following, that is also
false in real life:

Premises: If someone lives in Johannesburg, then he
lives in Tibet. If someone lives in Tibet, then he lives
in South America.

Correct Conclusion: If someone lives in Johannesburg,
then he lives in South America.

It should perhaps be mentioned that in non-mathematical
discussion tautological reasoning like the above is a
technique looked on with disfavour: to describe the arguments of a politician or social scientist as tautological is no compliment. Such a discription implies that
the person has advanced no substantial argument, but has
just **structured** it in such a way that the desired conclusion is forced from the **structure**. (Remember that
tautologies are statements which because of their structure, rather than their content, are always true).

## 20.    Who murdered Mr. Green?

"We have to rely solely on deduction. That to me,
makes the matter very much more interesting.
There is no routine work. It is a matter of the
intellect." - Hercule Poirot in Agatha Christie's
: "Murder on the Orient Express"

Using the laws so far developed we can now easily solve
the problem of who murdered Mr Green in the earlier
stated problem. For example,

Let    F represent "Fred murdered Mr Green"

       S represent "Sam murdered Mr Green"

       B represent "The butler was off Thursday night"

       P represent "Nurse Partridge witnessed the crime"

**A solution:**

| | | |
|---|---|---|
| 1. | F + S | Given |
| 2. | S $\Rightarrow$ B | Given |
| 3. | B $\Rightarrow$ $\bar{P}$ | Given |
| 4. | S $\Rightarrow$ $\bar{P}$ | Rule 4 on 2, 3 |
| 5. | P $\Rightarrow$ $\bar{S}$ | Rule 2 on 4 |
| 6. | P | Given |
| 7. | $\bar{S}$ | Rule 1 on 5, 6 |
| 8. | F | Rule 3 on 1, 7 |

That is to say, Fred is the guilty one.(Other orders of inference are also possible).

## 21.    Other examples in statement-reason form

Check the validity of the following two arguments by providing reasons.

(a)    If it rains or no-one comes, the party will be a failure. The party was not a failure. It couldn't have rained.

       Solution: The argument can be symbolized as:

$$(r + n) \Rightarrow f$$
$$\frac{\bar{f}}{\bar{r}}$$

49

```
Proof:  1.  (r + n) => f        Given
        2.  f̄                   Given
        3.  f̄ => ‾(r‾+‾n)        Rule 2 on 1, 2
        4.  ‾(r‾+‾n)             Rule 1 on 2, 3
        5.  r̄ . n̄               De Morgan on 4
        6.  r̄                   Definition of
                                conjunction (Valid)
```

(b)     q̄ => p
        p̄
        ─────
        q

```
Proof:  1.  q̄ => p             Given
        2.  p̄                   Given
        3.  p̄ => q              Rule 2 on 1
        4.  q                   Rule 1 on 2, 3 (Valid)
```

## 22.    Proof by Contradiction

"It is an old maxim of mine that when you have
excluded the impossible, whatever remains, however improbable, must be the truth" - Sherlock
Holmes in "The Beryl Coronet".


In a proof by contradiction (also known as "reductio ad
absurdum") the negation of the statement to be proved is
assumed to be true, and it is then shown that this assumption leads, by a series of otherwise correct procedures, to a statement known to be false. Usually, this
false statement is a contradiction - a statement of the
form (p . p̄) - which is necessarily always false. Now,
since all other procedures in the proof were correct, it
must have been the original assumption that led to the
contradiction, and therefore, the assumption is false.
If the assumption is false its negation - the original
statement - is true.

50

This method of proof is often used in our high school geometry., An example would be the usual proof of the converse of the following implication:

> "If a quadrilateral is cyclic, then its opposite angles are supplementary" (Can you recall why it is necessary to prove the converse, if the original implication is true?)

## Rule 5

This reasoning process, sometimes called the **Principle of Non-contradiction** may be symbolized in this way:

$[\bar{p} \Rightarrow (q \cdot \bar{q})] \Rightarrow p$

where p is the original statement and $\bar{p}$ is its assumed negation. It is left to the reader to verify that it is a tautology.

**Another example:**

Assume in the case of the murder of Mr Green that it is suspected that Fred is the culprit. Following is one version of an argument employing the principle of Non-Contradiction to show Fred as the guilty one.

| 1.  | F             | Statement to be proved |
|-----|---------------|------------------------|
| 2.  | $\bar{F}$     | Assumption |
| 3.  | F + S         | Given |
| 4.  | S             | Rule 3 on 2, 3 |
| 5.  | S ⇒ B         | Given |
| 6.  | B ⇒ $\bar{P}$ | Given |
| 7.  | S ⇒ $\bar{P}$ | Rule 4 on 5, 6 |
| 8.  | P ⇒ $\bar{S}$ | Rule 2 on 7 |
| 9.  | P             | Given |
| 10. | $\bar{S}$     | Rule 1 on 8, 9 |
| 11. | S . $\bar{S}$ | Definition of conjunction on 4, 10 |
| 12. | F             | Rule 5 on 2, 11 |

More precisely the contradiction-method to prove an implication of the form: p => q can be formulated as follows:

1.    Assume p to be true.

2.    Assume q (the conclusion) to be false.

3.    Show that this leads to a contradiction.

This can be symbolized as

(p . $\bar{q}$ => r . $\bar{r}$) => (p => q)

(It is left to the reader to establish that it is a tautology.)

**Example:**

**To prove:**

If n is an integer and $n^2$ is even, then n is even.

52

**Proof:**

1.    Assume p: n is an integer and $n^2$ is even.

2.    Assume $\bar{q}$: n is not even ... so, n is odd.


Since n is odd, by the definition of an odd integer, it follows that

n = 2p + 1 for some integer p          ... (a)


To see that $n^2$ is an odd integer, square both sides of (a) to obtain

$n^2 = (2p + 1)^2 = 4p^2 + 4p + 1$          ... (b)


By rewriting (b) we get

$n^2 = 2 (2p^2 + 2p) + 1$          ... (c)


Thus, $n^2 = 2k + 1$, where $k = 2p^2 + p$, and so by defini-tion, $n^2$ is odd. On the other hand, in the first assumption, it clearly states that $n^2$ is even. Thus, $n^2$ is both odd and even, and this contradiction establishes the proof.


In most cases, the contradiction is achieved by deriving a contradiction to the given or assumed hypothesis p. Upon close analysis, one can see that in such cases we are really proving that "not q" leads to "not p", which is the contrapositive of the original implication. Therefore in these cases, the contradiction-method can also be viewed to be simply based on the logical equivalence between an implication and its contrapositive (See Rule 2). Generally, however, when one uses the contradiction-method one does not necessarily know beforehand what the contradiction is going to be. It may be of the form p.$\bar{p}$, but it may also be some other form of contradiction with something else that we know is true.

As a general rule, use contradiction when the statement "not q" gives you some useful information. There are at least two such recognizable cases:

(i)     when statement q is one of only two possible cases (e.g. the previous example where the integer n could only be odd or even)

(ii)    when statement q contains the key words "no", "never" or "not" in it (see later exercise).

## 23.    Proof by Counter-example

"I never make exceptions, An exception disproves the rule" - Sherlock Holmes in "The Sign of Four".

This is a method used for proving that a conjecture is false. Consider for example the conjecture that: "If n is a prime, than $2^3 - 1$ also has to be a prime." Checking this conjecture inductively we find:

$2^2 - 1 = 3 \quad 2^3 - 1 = 7 \quad 2^5 - 1 = 31 \quad 2^7 - 1 = 127$

All these cases support the conjecture. However, $2^{11} - 1 = 2047$ is not a prime as 2047 is divisible by 23. By providing a **counter-example** we have shown that the conjecture cannot be true, and that it is false. Logically, this argument is of course based on the fact that a statement (p) and its negation ($\bar{p}$) cannot both be true. (p. $\bar{p}$ is a contradiction). Since we have shown $\bar{p}$ to be true, p has to be false.

## 24.    Mathematical Induction

In the above example we were lucky to have the fifth case contradict our conjecture. It is however not always so easy finding a counter-example. For instance mathematicians have been searching for ages for a formula which would help to generate prime numbers. About 500 BC Chinese mathematicians conjectured that if $2^n - 2$ is divisible by n, then n must be prime. If this were true it would have been a great boon for the establishment of the primality of a number, as then one would only have to carry out the division of $2^n - 2$ by n. Approaching the conjecture inductively, one finds that: $2^3 - 2$, $2^5 - 2$, $2^7 - 2$ are divisible by the primes 3, 5 and 7, but $2^4 - 2$, $2^6 - 2$, $2^8 - 2$ are not divisible by the composite numbers, 4, 6 and 8.

It turns out that the empirical investigation supports the conjecture up to $2^{340} - 2$. In all these cases $2^n - 2$ is divisible by n when n is prime, and not divisible by n when it is composite. However, $n^{341} - 2$ is divisible by 341 even though 341 is composite, as 341 = 11 x 31. So the conjecture was not true!

Let's assume that we are studying the problem of finding the total number of squares (of any size) on an 8 x 8 chessboard, and from this analysis we make the following remarkable discovery (after generalizing and deriving a formula), namely that the sum of n squares of consecutive numbers can be expressed in a formula as follows:

$$1^2 + 2^2 + 3^2 + \ldots + n^2 = \frac{n(n + 1)(2n + 1)}{6}$$

How then can we prove that a conjecture like this is in general always true? If the set of natural numbers were **finite**, we could of course set out to check all the possibilities (a method of proof often used, and called exhausting all possibilities). But since the set of natural numbers is **infinite**, this is obviously an impossible task.

Faced with proving similar problems, mathematicians invented a marvellous method of proof, referred to as **mathematical induction**. This method can be formulated as follows:

Let P (n) be a statement for a certain set of natural numbers:

If:   (i) P (m) is true, **and**

      (ii) for all k ≥ m the **assumption** that P (k) is true, implies that P (k + 1) is true.

Then P (n) is true for all natural numbers of n ≥ m. (In most problems the value of m = 1)

The main argument of mathematical induction can be symbolically represented as:

$$[P(m) \cdot (P(k) \Rightarrow P(k + 1))] \Rightarrow P(m + 1)$$

A basic conceptual stumbling block for many people are their uneasiness about the second step in mathematical induction. "How can you establish the truth of P (k + 1) if you don't even know if P (k) is true?" is a question often asked.

The essential argument on which mathematical induction is based, is of course the Law of Detachment stated in symbols: $[p \cdot (p \Rightarrow q)] \Rightarrow q$

In the part $p \Rightarrow q$ we do not have to know at all yet the truth of p. What interests us only is that q follows from p. Having proved that the general implication P (k) $\Rightarrow$ P (k + 1) is true (for k ≥ m), and knowing P (m) to be true, we invoke the Law of Detachment to conclude that P (m + 1) will also be true. Since we have now proved P (m + 1) to be true, we can invoke the general implication P (k) $\Rightarrow$ P (k + 1) to show that P (m + 2) will also be true. By repeated application of the general implication, it should be clear that P (m + 3), P (m + 4) ... will be true, and in general P (n). (The assumption that we can apply the general implication "ad infinitum" is of course an axiom.)

57

# 25.  Quantifiers

A statement in mathematics like $2x + 3 = x + 1$ is not a proposition, because it cannot be said to be either true or false. Such statements are often described as **propositional forms**. The more familiar way is to say that they are **open sentences**, because they present "open questions" since the variable $x$ is open for replacement by any value in its domain. It is only when $x$ values from the domain are put into an open sentence, that it becomes a proposition which can be either true or false. For instance, substituting $x = 2$ into the open sentence above, would transform it into a false proposition.

Now this equation (open sentence) consists of two expressions, namely $2x + 3$ and $x + 1$, whose output values change as the input values ($x$) are changed. Now it happens that only for a certain value of x, namely $-2$, the two expressions give the same output value, namely $-1$. The open sentence $2x + 3 = x + 1$ is therefore only true for one value of x.

However, there are certain types of equations like $2x + 3x = 5x$ that consist of two expressions $2x + 3x$ and $5x$ which always give the same output values for the same input values, no matter what values of x are chosen. As pointed out earlier, when this happens, we say that two such expressions are equivalent and that the equation represents an **identity** which is true for all values of x.

Now from a logical point of view this distinction between types of equations is approached as follows. An
open sentence that has the same **truth values** for all re-
placements of the variable is said to be **universally
quantified** and may be expressed using a universal quantifier such as "All", "For all x", "every", or the symbol $\forall_x$.

A statement which is meant to apply to at least one
(possibly every) replacement of the variable is said to
be **existentially quantified** and may be expressed using
an existential quantifier such as "Some", "For some x",
"There exists an x such that", "At least one", or the
symbol $\exists_x$. Examples of statements that are universally
quantified:

(i)     $\forall_x$ 2x + 3x = 5x

(ii)    All rectangles are parallelograms

(iii)   $\forall_{x \in Z}$ x + 2 = x, where Z is the set of integers
        (This universally quantified statement is false)

Examples of statements that are existentially quantified:

(i)     $\exists_x$ x + 2 = 3

(ii)    Some integers are divisible by 3

(iii)   $\exists_{x \in Z}$ x is divisible by 3.

To show that a universally quantified statement is false, it is sufficient to find a counter-example for which the original statement is false. Example:

$$\forall_x x^2 > 0 \text{ is false, because } x = 0 \Rightarrow x^2 \not> 0.$$

To show that an existentially quantified statement is false, it is necessary to demonstrate that there are no cases for which the original statement is true. Example:

$$\exists_x x^2 < 0 \text{ is not true.}$$ To prove this we either have to show that there are no x for which it is true, or that it's negation $\forall_x x^2 \not< 0$ is always true.

Note that the negation of a universally quantified statement is an existentially quantified statement, and vice versa. For example, the negation of the proposition "All men are mortal" reads "It is not true that all men are mortal" or "all men are not mortal". In other words, there exists at least one man who is not mortal. (Remember that a statement P and its negation $\overline{P}$ cannot both be true. If the one is true, the other is false). Symbolically, then, if M denotes the set of men, then the above can be written as:

$$\overline{\forall x \in M; (x \text{ is mortal})} \Leftrightarrow \exists x \in M; (x \text{ is not mortal})$$

Generally, it can be written as:

$$\overline{\forall x \in A; p(x)} \Leftrightarrow \exists x \in A; \overline{p(x)}$$

In other words, the statement:

"It is not true that, for every x∈A, p(x) is true" is equivalent to:

"There exists an x∈A such that p(x) is false"

Obviously the following also holds:

$$\overline{\exists x \in A; \ p(x)} \ <=> \ \forall x \in A; \ \overline{p(x)}$$

Therefore, the statement:

"It is not true that there exists an x∈A such that p(x) is true" is equivalent to:

"For all x∈A, p(x) is false"

Examples:

(i)    The negation of the true statement: $\exists_x \ x + 3 = 10$ for the real numbers, is $\forall_x, \ x + 3 \neq 10$.

(ii)   The negation of the false statement: $\forall_x, \ x + 3 < 10$ for the real numbers, is $\exists_x, \ x + 3 \geq 10$.

**Multiple quantification** can occur when two or more variables are concerned, for example

1.    $\forall_x \ \forall_y \ xy = yx$ would mean "For all x and for all y, xy = yx."

2.    $\forall_x \ \exists_y \ y < x$ would mean "For each and every x, there exists a y such that y < x"

61

# 26.   Equivalent equations, identities and proofs with equivalence

In the solution of mathematical equations we frequently utilize the concept of equivalence. As previously said, two algebraic expressions are equivalent if for the same input values of x they produce the same output values. Thus, one could say

$\forall_x$, 2x + x <=> 3x

Similarly, two equations are equivalent if they have the same solution set. Thus, one could say

$$\frac{2x + x}{3} = 12 <=> 2x + x = 36$$

We can therefore use equivalence to solve an equation like the one below by using appropriate algebraic manipulation and constructing progressively simpler equivalent equations until the solution set becomes obvious.

$$\frac{2x + x}{3} = 12$$

<=>    2x + x  = 36
<=>       3x  = 36
<=>        x  = 12

Now since the statements are all equivalent and 12 is obviously the solution set of the last statement, it immediately implies (reasoning backwards) that it is also the solution of the third, second and first statement. Strictly speaking, therefore, when using equivalence it is totally unnecessary to "test" the last statement's

solution set by substitution in the first statement. Remember that the equivalence between two equations, e.g.

$A = B \iff C = D$

also means that $A = B$ **implies** that $C = D$, and **vice
versa.**

However, not all algebraic manipulations necessarily
transform equations into alternative equivalent equations. For instance, squaring both sides of the equation
$x = 3$ produces $x^2 = 9$, which is **not** equivalent to the
first equation, since the latter could also have the solution $x = -3$. Thus, $x = 3$ implies $x^2 = 9$, but is **not** implied by $x^2 = 9$. We therefore have a one-way implication
which can be written as

$$\implies \quad \begin{matrix} x = 3 \\ x^2 = 9 \end{matrix}$$

Now this distinction is of cardinal importance when
solving equations. For instance, consider carefully the
argument set out in the statements below. Are all the
equations equivalent?

$$x + \sqrt{5 - x} + 1 = 0$$
$$x + 1 = \sqrt{5 - x}$$
$$(x + 1)^2 = 5 - x$$
$$x^2 + 3x - 4 = 0$$
$$(x - 1)(x + 4) = 0$$
$$x = 1 \text{ or } x = -4$$

Quite clearly the two equations $x + 1 = -\sqrt{5 - x}$ and
$(x + 1)^2 = 5 - x$ are not equivalent. The first implies
the second, but not vice versa. In such cases, it is
therefore absolutely essential to test the final solutions by substitution into the original equation. (Note

63

that using the symbol $\therefore$ or the term "therefore" in solving equations, **logically compels** you to **test all solutions.**)

Consider the argument below. What is wrong with it?

$$\frac{x}{x + 2} - \frac{4}{x + 1} = \frac{-2}{x + 2} \quad \ldots (1)$$

$$\Leftrightarrow \quad \frac{x(x+1) - 4(x+2)}{(x+2)(x+1)} = \frac{-2(x+1)}{(x+2)(x+1)} \quad \ldots (2)$$
$$\Leftrightarrow \quad x^2 + x - 4x - 8 = -2x - 2 \quad \ldots (3)$$
$$\Leftrightarrow \quad x^2 - x - 6 = 0 \quad \ldots (4)$$
$$\Leftrightarrow \quad (x - 3)(x + 2) = 0 \quad \ldots (5)$$
$$\Leftrightarrow \quad x = 3 \text{ or } x = -2 \quad \ldots (6)$$

Clearly equation (2) and (3) are not equivalent, since $x = -2$ and $x = -1$ are **excluded** from the solution set of (2) (division by zero is not allowed), but not necessarily in (3). To maintain the equivalence between equations, it should    be rewritten as

$$\frac{x}{x + 2} - \frac{4}{x + 1} = \frac{-2}{x + 2} \; ; \; x \neq -1 \text{ or } -2 \quad \ldots (1)$$

$$\frac{x(x=1) - 4(x+2)}{(x+2)(x+1)} = \frac{-2(x+4)}{(x+2)(x+1)} \; ; \; x \neq -1 \text{ or } -2 \quad \ldots (2)$$
$$\Leftrightarrow \quad x^2 + x - 4x - 8 = 2x - 2; \; x \neq -1 \text{ or } -2 \quad \ldots (3)$$
$$\Leftrightarrow \quad x^2 - x - 6 = 0; \qquad x \neq -1 \text{ or } -2 \quad \ldots (4)$$
$$\Leftrightarrow \quad (x - 3)(x + 2) = 0; \qquad x \neq -1 \text{ or } -2 \quad \ldots (5)$$
$$\Leftrightarrow \quad x = 3 \text{ or } x = -2; \qquad x \neq -1 \text{ or } -2 \quad \ldots (6)$$
$$\Leftrightarrow \quad x = 3 \quad \ldots (7)$$

Another way of rewriting it, is to just use the implication sign $\Rightarrow$ next to equation 3, and just remembering to test the solution of equation (6) in the original statement. The above setting out of the argument, however is to be preferred because it automatically eliminates the necessity of testing.

It is always important during the solution of equations to bear the maintenance of equivalence between equations in mind. For another example, consider the equation $x^3=x^2$ which can be divided both sides by $x^2$ to obtain x=1. The equation $x^3=x^2$ is however **not** equivalent to x=1, since the former could also have the solution x=0. To maintain equivalence, $x^3=x^2$ should be transformed to $x^3-x^2=0$ and then factorised. (As a rule one should always beware of multiplying or dividing equations with expressions that could be zero, since this can effect the equivalence of the equations involved.)

Equivalence of equations is also useful in proving mathematical identities. In order to prove that a given equation is an identity, we may use standard algebraic processes to show that it is equivalent to a known or accepted identity.

**Example:**

**Prove the identity:**

$$\frac{\sin^2 x}{1 - \cos x} = 1 + \cos x$$

**Proof:**

$$\frac{\sin^2 x}{1 - \cos x} = 1 + \cos x; \quad \cos x \ne 1 <=> x \ne 0^\circ \pm n \cdot 360^\circ$$

$$<=> \sin^2 x = 1 - \cos^2 x; \quad \cos x \ne 1 <=> x \ne 0^\circ \pm n \cdot 360^\circ$$
$$<=> \sin^2 x = \sin^2 x; \quad \cos x \ne 1 <=> x \ne 0^\circ \pm n \cdot 360^\circ$$

which is an obvious identity and completes the proof.

## Discussion:

Note that the above equations are all equivalent only if the restriction $x \neq 0° \pm n \cdot 360°$ is placed throughout. Therefore, leaving out this restriction would invalidate the proof. Furthermore, using the term "therefore", or the symbols $\therefore$ and $\Rightarrow$ instead of equivalence $\Leftrightarrow$, would also invalidate the proof. The reason simply being that these symbols have only a one-way meaning. Therefore, all you have shown if you use these symbols in the proof above, is that if the identity to prove is true, then the identity $\sin^2 x = \sin^2 x$ would also be true. Meanwhile the converse, which you were supposed to prove remains unproven.

Another way of putting it, is to say that the truth of an implication $p \Rightarrow q$ as well as the truth of q, **do not necessarily guarantee** the truth of p (see the truth table definition). An example to illustrate this is the following.

Let p: $2 = -2$
Square both sides to obtain:
    q: $4 = 4$

Clearly the implication $p \Rightarrow q$ is true as well as q, but certainly not p! (Also note that $[(p \Rightarrow q) \cdot q] \Rightarrow p$ is not a tautology). If you therefore desire to exclusively use the implication symbol $\Rightarrow$ in the previous example you are logically compelled to start with the last statement which is clearly **true** and reverse your reasoning until you arrive at the identity to be proved.

Of course, another way to prove that it is an identity is to start on the left hand side of the equation and to manipulate the expression until the right hand side is obtained, or vice versa. However, this often (but not always) tends to be more cumbersome than using equivalence.

Equivalence can also sometimes be useful as a method of proof in geometry as shown in the example below.

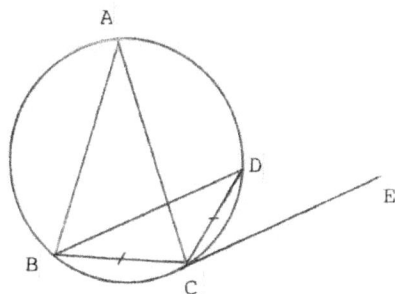

CE is a tangent to the circle.

**To prove:** $B\hat{A}C = D\hat{C}E$

**Proof:** $B\hat{A}C = D\hat{C}E$

$\Longleftrightarrow B\hat{D}C = D\hat{C}E$ ... $B\hat{A}C = B\hat{D}C$ on chord BC

$\Longleftrightarrow C\hat{B}D = D\hat{C}E$ ... $BC = DC \Longleftrightarrow C\hat{B}D = B\hat{D}C$

which is true according to the alternate segment theorem, and completes the proof.

# Discussion

On first sight this argument may seem invalid. But consider the first two lines of the proof. It says first of
all:

"If $B\hat{A}C = D\hat{C}E$ (and $B\hat{A}C = B\hat{D}C$), then $B\hat{D}C = D\hat{C}E$"

which is clearly valid. Secondly, it says:

"If $B\hat{D}C = D\hat{C}E$ (and $B\hat{A}C = B\hat{D}C$), then $B\hat{A}C = D\hat{C}E$"

which is the first one's converse, and clearly also
valid. Now if an implication and its converse are both
valid, it means that they are equivalent. The same can
be said for the second and third lines of the proof.

This method of proof is more economical than the traditional method of proof which only uses one-way implication =>. In the traditional method we frequently dis-
cover the proof by a **backward analysis** from that which
is **asked to that which is given.** However, since conven-
tionally implications are used, the written down proof
must logically proceed **forward** (in the **reverse** direction
to the initial analysis), from that which is **given** to
that which is **asked.** But using equivalence as in the example above, eliminates the necessity of **reversing** the
line of argument, since that is automatically done by
using the equivalence symbol.

Furthermore, using this method correctly shows either of
two things. Firstly, it may automatically show that the

converse of the implication p => q is also valid. Or in such cases where this is not possible, it shows that the implication being proved is equivalent to some other implication.

Unfortunately this method in geometry is often logically complicated to always employ correctly, especially if the argument is long and there are statements involved in the reasoning that are only one-way implications. Consequently it is a generally accepted convention that geometric proofs are preferably written using one-way implications. In this way the chances of making logical errors are smaller. One can, of course, alternatively do the analysis as in the example above, but using the symbol <= instead of equivalence.

## 27.   Exercise

1.     Decide by truth tables which of the following arguments are valid. Assume in each case the following implication as given: "If Johnny is telling the truth, then his father does not punish him."

(a)    His father does not punish him. Therefore Johnny is telling the truth.

(b)    Johnny is telling the truth. Therefore his father does not punish him.

(c)    His father does punish him. Therefore Johnny is not telling the truth.

(d)    Johnny is not telling the truth. Therefore his father does punish him.

2.  If this figure is regular then its sides are
    equal. If this figure is a hexagon then it is
    regular. This figure does not have equal sides.
    Can we infer that this figure is not a hexagon?

3.  Decide by truth tables which of the following
    arguments are valid. Assume the following impli-
    cation in each case: "If this quadrilateral has
    at least one pair of parallel sides, then it is
    a trapezium."

    (a)  This quadrilateral has only one pair of
         parallel sides. Therefore this quadrila-
         teral is a trapezium.

    (b)  It is a trapezium. Therefore this quadri-
         lateral has at least one pair of parallel
         sides.

    (c)  This quadrilateral does not have only one
         pair of parallel sides. Therefore it is
         not a trapezium.

4.  A certain company claims the following:

    (a)  "If you use Stay-hair, your hair will not
         fall out."

         Under what circumstances will you be able
         to take them to court for false claims?

    (b)  A doctor says to a patient:

         "If you do not have this operation, you
         will never walk again."

         The patient declines to have himself ope-
         rated upon, but nevertheless recovers
         sufficiently to walk unsupported. Was the
         doctor's diagnosis wrong?

70

(c)     Your teacher says:

"You may read **Elementary Logic** only if
you have finished your quadratic equations."

Are you logically obliged to first finish
your quadratic equations before you may
read this book?

5.      Check the validity of the following arguments
either by giving reasons or by constructing
truth tables. Where it is of interest, comment
on the actual truth or falsity of the premisses
or conclusions.

(a)     Either that figure is called a dipteron,
or it is called a diphrion. It is not a
dipteron, so it must be a diphrion.

(b)     If a person is young, then he is not very
sensible. Now I am not young, so I must
be very sensible.

(c)     If $x > 4$, then $x^2 > 16$. But $x^2 > 16$, so $x > 4$.

(d)     If $x^2 = 9$, then either $x = 3$ or $= -3$; but
$x \neq 3$, so $x = -3$.

(e)     If $x$ is an insect, then $x$ does not have
eight legs. If $x$ is a spider, then $x$ has
eight legs. If $x$ is a spider, then $x$ is
not an insect.

(f)     It is not possible for a number to be
both prime and a multiple of three. This
number is prime. It cannot be a multiple
of three.

(g)     If we send money to those countries that
need it, then they will industrialize. If
they industrialize, then they will com-

71

pete for our markets. If they do that, we shall become poor. We must not become poor. So we must not send money to those countries that need it.

(h)     If a function f(x) has a (local) minimum, say at x = a, then f'(a) = 0. Since it is given that f' (b) = 0, the function has a (local) minimum at x = b.

(i)     If a function f(x) has a (local) minimum, say at x = a, then f'(a) = 0. This function does not have a (local) minimum. Therefore f'(x) will be zero for no value of x.

(j)     Communists are opposed to the government and want to violently overthrow it. John is opposed to the government, and is therefore a communist who wants to violently overthrow the government.

(k)     Blacks want full participation in the political system of the country at the highest level. Jennie is white, and therefore does not want blacks to have full participation in the political system of the country.

(l)     A common language, religion and culture, and not race, determines group identity. Persons A and B do not have a common language, religion and culture, but are of the same race. Nonetheless, persons A and B have the same group identity.

(m)     If there were any truth about flying saucers, the Air Force would certainly deny it. So there must be something to the rumours because they certainly deny it.

(n)     I guess Smith is not going to graduate this year. if he does not satisfy the language requirement he can't graduate, and he is not planning to do anything to meet the requirement.

6.(a) In a previous exercise we showed that the law of the Contrapositive was equivalent to $(\bar{p} + q)$ as well as $\overline{(p \cdot \bar{q})}$. Use this fact to prove the implication: "if $\overline{(p \cdot q)}$, then $p = >\bar{q}$."

(b) Now use the above to show that the argument

$\overline{p.q}$
$\underline{p}$
$\bar{q}$

is valid.

(It is often very useful to employ equivalent forms of the law of the contrapositive as in 6(a) above.)

7. There is a rule called **Modus Tollens**, which states that if an implication is true and its conclusion is false, then its hypothesis is also false.

(a) Symbolize this rule.

(b) Prove by using truth tables that it is a tautology.

(c) Show that this rule can be deduced from the laws of Detachment and Contrapositive.

(d) Analyse the following line of reasoning: On arriving at the darkened home of

friends, one thinks, "They aren't home".
On what rule(s) is this reasoning based?

(e)     Give some of your own examples of **Modus Tollens.**

8.      Check the validity of the following arguments by giving reasons.

(a)   $(p \Rightarrow \bar{q}) \Rightarrow r$
$$\frac{\bar{r}}{p.q}$$

(b)   $\frac{[(p \Rightarrow q) \cdot r]}{\frac{p \Rightarrow q}{r}}$

(c)   $(p + q) \Rightarrow (r \cdot \bar{s})$
$$\frac{p}{r + s}$$

9.      In the next couple of questions (i)-(xiv), use the methods of the previous examples to draw conclusions from the given premises. If no conclusion can be reached, say so. Where it is of interest, comment upon the actual truth or falsity of the premises and conclusion.

(i)     If the mathematical structure contains no identity element, then it cannot be a group. This structure is not a group. So ...

(ii)    I told him that if he worked hard or had a great deal of luck, he would pass his exams. He did not pass them. So ...

(iii)   So called "possession of devils" is either an example of mental derangement or it really is the effect of some supernatural power. I'm certain that it is an example of mental derangement. So ...

74

(iv)    It is not true that if he lies, then he
        is guilty. Either he is guilty, or his
        sister is. So ..

(v)     All rectangles are cyclic quadrilaterals.
        This figure is not a cyclic quadrila-
        teral. So ...

(vi)    If there are more blacks than whites in
        the country, there should be more black
        students at university than white stu-
        dents. There are more blacks than whites
        in the country. So ...

(vii)   If he is elected, he will revive the
        economy and ensure our national security.
        He is not elected. So ...

(viii)  The economical situation will only im-
        prove if the political situation im-
        proves. The political situation improves.
        So ...

(ix)    Two triangles are similar if, and only
        if, corresponding sides are proportional.
        These two triangles' sides are propor-
        tional. So ...

(x)     If there are the same number of women as
        men in the population, there should be as
        many women as men in senior managerial
        positions. There are less women than men
        in senior positions. So ...

(xi)    If a figure is a three-legged trapezium
        (three sides equal), it is an isosceles
        trapezium. All isosceles trapeziums are
        cyclic. If a figure is a cyclic quadri-
        lateral, its opposite angles are supple-
        mentary. This figure is a three-legged
        trapezium. So ...

(xii)   A number is either prime or composite.
        This number is not prime. So ...

75

(xiii) If one works hard, one will pass. He failed. So ...

(xiv) If one is intelligent, one will pass. He is intelligent. So ...

10. In each section:

(a) state every sentence in symbols;

(b) state the negation of each first sentence in words;

(c) state which sentences are equivalent.

(i) $3x - 7 = 5$ if and only if $x = 4$

$3x - 7 = 5$ is a sufficient and necessary condition that $x = 4$

$x = 4$ is a sufficient condition that $3x - 7 = 5$

If $x = 4$, then $3x - 7 = 5$

(ii) A structure is a group only if it has an identity element.

The existence of an identity element is a necessary condition for the structure to be a group.

That a structure is a group is a sufficient condition for it to have an identity element.

(iii) If a plane figure is transformed by an isometric transformation, then the transformed figure is congruent to the original figure.

If congruency of a plane figure is invariant (maintained) under a transformation, then that transformation is an isometric transformation.

Congruency is maintained under a transformation only if that transformation is
an isometry.

11.   Investigate the validity of the following three
conjectures.

(a)   The formula $6x - 1$ gives prime numbers
for $x = 1, 2, 3 \ldots$

(b)   The formula $n^2 - n + 41$ gives prime numbers for $n = 1, 2, 3 \ldots$

(c)   If m and n are odd integers, then mn is
an odd integer.

If true, prove it. If not, provide a counter-example.

12.   Derive a formula to determine the sum of the
first n positive integers (hint: use a table),
and prove that the formula is generally valid.

13.   Prove the following conjectures.

(a)   There is no largest prime number.

(b)   $\sqrt{2}$ is not a rational number which can be
expressed as p/q where both p and q are
integers.

(c)   If the lines R and S are both perpendicular to T, then R and S are parallel.

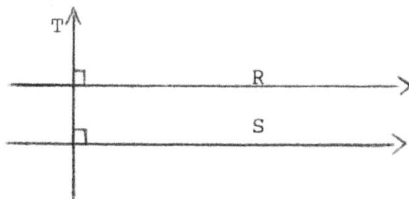

14.(a)  Study the following pattern.

$$1 + 3 = 4$$
$$1 + 3 + 5 = 9$$
$$1 + 3 + 5 + 7 = 16$$
$$1 + 3 + 5 + 7 + 9 = ?$$

Formulate a conjecture in appropriate symbols and prove it.

(b)  (i) Compute

$$1^3 + 2^3 + 3^3 + 4^3 + \ldots + 100^3 \text{ (Find a short cut)}$$

(ii) Now write down a formula for computing
$$1^3 + 2^3 + 3^3 + \ldots + n^3$$

(iii) Prove that the formula is correct

(c)  Prove that $1^2 + 2^2 + 3^2 + 3^2 \ldots$
$$+ n^2 = \frac{n(n+1)(2n+1)}{6}$$

15.(a)  Say which of the following statements are universally quantified, existentially quantified as well as which are false.

(i)  $\forall_{x \in z}$ $2x + 1 = 4$ where $Z$ is the set of integers.

(ii)  No elephant is green.

(iii)  Not all animals are like you.

(iv)  None of the powers of 2 is divisible by 5.

(v)    There exists an integer x such that x is divisible by 3.

(vi)   $\exists_x$ sin 2x = 2 sin x cos x

(vii)  $\forall_x$ sin 2x = 2 sin x cos x

(b)  Say what is meant by the following, and say whether it is true or false.

(i)    $\forall_x \forall_y$ x + y > 1 with both x and y in the domain 1, 2, 3, 4, 5

(ii)   $\exists_x \exists_y$ x + y = 1 with both x and y in the domain 1, 2, 3,4,5

(iii)  $\exists_y \forall_x$ y < x with both x and y in the domain of the integers.

(c)  Quantify the following statements

(i)    tan x = sin x/cos x

(ii)   yx = 9

(iii)  y = $^9/_x$

(iv)   (x − 3)$^2$ + y$^2$ = 16 with both x and y in the domain of the integers.

(v)    log x + log x = log x$^2$

(vi)   sec x = $^1/_{\cos x}$

(vii)  y = $\pm\sqrt{x + 1}$

(viii) y = |x|

(ix)   $^1/_2$ cos 2x = cos x

16.(a)  Determine the truth value of each of the following statements. (Here the universal set is the set of real numbers).

(i) $\forall_x$, $|x| = x$      (ii) $\exists_x$, $x^2 = x$

(iii) $\forall_x$, $x + 1 > x$      (iv) $\exists_x$, $x + 2 = x$

(v) $\exists_x$, $|x| = 0$      (vi) $\forall_x$, $2x > x + 2$

(vii) $\exists_x$, $\log^2 x \geq 2 \log x$      (viii) $\exists_x$, $\cos x = x$

(ix) $\forall_a \forall_b$, $a + b = b + a$      (x) $\exists_x$, $\sin x > \tan x$

(b)      Negate each of the statements in (a)

17.      Analyse the logical structure of the following proof. Is the logical structure valid? Supply reasons for your answer

**To prove:**

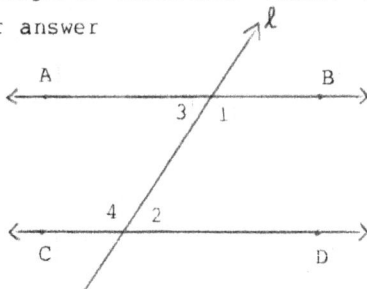

If lines AB and CD never cross each other, then the co-interior angles formed by the transversal $\ell$, are supplementary (e.g. $\hat{1} + \hat{2} = 180^\circ$).

**Proof:**

Assume $\hat{1} + \hat{2} < 180^\circ$

Then a triangle can be formed by extending AB and CD to O, and the two lines therefore intersect. (The sum of 3 angles of a triangle = $180^\circ$.)

80

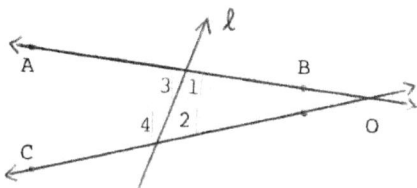

Similarly it can be shown that if $\overset{\wedge}{1} + \overset{\wedge}{2} > 180°$, then $\overset{\wedge}{3} + \overset{\wedge}{4} < 180°$, and AB and CD will intersect each other on the other side of the transversal $\ell$. Thus, $\overset{\wedge}{1} + \overset{\wedge}{2} = 180°$ and completes the proof.

18.  Is it a sufficient condition for a quadrilateral to be a parallelogram to have one pair of opposite sides and one pair of opposite angles equal? If so, provide reasons. If not, draw or accurately construct a counter-example.

19.  Negate each of the following statements:

(i)  If there is a riot, then someone is killed.

(ii)  If the teacher is absent, then some students do not complete their homework.

(iii)  It is daylight and all the people have risen.

(iv)  All rectangles are parallelograms.

(v)  There are some trapeziums that are cyclic.

20.  Combine each of the following into one statement:

(i)  The theorem of Pythagoras and its converse.

(ii)   "The exterior angle of a cyclic quadrilateral is equal to the interior opposite
angle" and "If the exterior angle of a
quadrilateral is equal to the opposite
interior angle, then the quadrilateral is
cyclic."

(iii)   "If $x = \alpha$ and $x = \beta$ are the roots of a
quadratic equation, then $(x - \alpha)(x - \beta)$
$= 0$" and "If $(x - \alpha)(x - \beta) = 0$, then $x$
$= \alpha$ and $x = \beta$ are the roots of the
quadratic equation."

(iv)   "If the diagonals of a quadrilateral bisect each other the quadrilateral is a
parallelogram" and "The diagonals of a
parallelogram bisect each other".

(v)   "If $x + 2 = 0$, then $x = -2$" and "If $x = -2$, then $x + 2 = 0$"

21.   Connect the midpoints of the sides of any
quadrilateral.

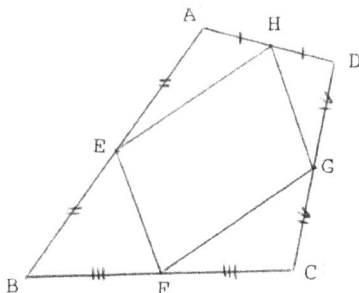

What type of quadrilateral is EFGH? Investigate
some more cases to verify your hypothesis. Try
and prove it and then answer the following related questions by filling in the missing parts.
(Do not answer them too hastily - the questions

82

are not as simple as they look. Some questions also have more than one correct answer).

(a) It is a sufficient condition that the midpoints of a ........ are connected so that a rectangle is formed in the middle.

(b) It is a ........ condition that the midpoints of a ........ are connected so that a rhombus is formed in the middle.

(c) For the circumscribed quadrilateral ABCD to be a square, it is a ........ condition that the inscribed quadrilateral EFGH is a square.

(d) For the circumscribed quadrilateral ABCD to be a rectangle, it is a necessary, but not sufficient, condition that the inscribed quadrilateral EFGH is a ........

(e) For the circumscribed quadrilateral ABCD to be a kite, it is a ........ condition that the inscribed quadrilateral EFGH is a ........

(f) It is a necessary and a sufficient condition that the midpoints of a quadrilateral with the property that ........ be connected to form a rectangle in the middle.

(g) For the circumscribed quadrilateral ABCD to have equal diagonals, it is a necessary and sufficient condition that the inscribed quadrilateral EFGH is a ........

(h) Give reasons for your answers above.

22. Prove that all the angles of an equilateral triangle are equal. Then show the logical structure on which your proof is based.

23.    Analyse the logical structure of a textbook proof of the implication "The angle in a semi-circle is a right angle".

24.    Prove the following conjecture.

"Two lines AB and CD intersect each other in O such that the products of the line segments are equal (AO . OB = CO . OD) if, and only if, the points A, B, C and D lie on the circumference of a circle."

Show the logical structure on which your proof is based.

25.    Carefully analyse the proof below. Is it valid?

**To proof:** If ABCD is a cyclic quadrilateral, then the exterior angle DCE is equal to the opposite interior angle A.

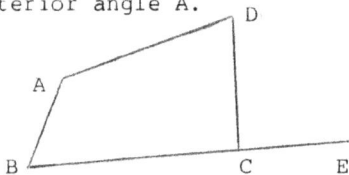

**Proof:**    $D\hat{C}E = \hat{A}$

$<=>\ \hat{A} + B\hat{C}D = 180^{\circ} \ \ldots \ D\hat{C}E + B\hat{C}D = 180^{\circ}$
$\qquad\qquad\qquad\qquad\qquad\qquad$ (straight line)

which is true according to the theorem which states that "ABCD is a cyclic quadrilateral if, and only if, $\hat{A}$ + B$\hat{C}$D = 180°". This completes the proof of the given implication, as well as its converse.

How would the validity of the proof be affected if the phrase "if, and only if" in the theorem in the last step, were to be replaced by the phrase "only if."?

26.     Prove the following theorems using the method of equivalence.

   (a)     The sum of the angles of a triangle is equal to 180°

   (b)     A line through a point on the circumference of a circle is a tangent to the circle if, and only if, the angle between the line and a chord through the point is equal to the angle in the alternate segment.

Since the argument in (a) is based on equivalence, reformulate (a) using the phrase "if and only if". Compare the proof of (a) with (b). What is the essential difference between them?

27.     Correct the proof below:

**To prove:**

$$\frac{1 - \sin x}{\cos x} = \frac{\cos x}{1 + \sin x}$$

**Proof:**

$$\frac{1 - \sin x}{\cos x} = \frac{\cos x}{1 + \sin x}$$

$$\Rightarrow 1 - \sin^2 x = \cos^2 x$$
$$\Rightarrow \cos^2 x = \cos^2 x$$

28.   Fill in the appropriate symbols in the solution of the equation below (and complete it).

$$2\sqrt{x + 4} - x = 1$$
$$2\sqrt{x + 4} = x + 1$$
$$4(x + 4) = x^2 + 2x + 1$$
$$x^2 - 2x - 15 = 0$$
$$(x - 5)(x + 3) = 0$$
$$x = 5 \text{ or } x = -3$$

29.   What is missing in the following argument for solving a trigonometrical equation to make it completely logically acceptable?

$$2\sin^2 x - \sin x = 0$$
$$\Leftrightarrow \sin x(2\sin x - 1) = 0$$
$$\Leftrightarrow \sin x = 0 \text{ o } \sin x = {}^1\!/_2$$
$$\Leftrightarrow x = 0^\circ \text{ or } x = 30^\circ \text{ or } x = 150^\circ$$

Explain why leaving this out creates a logical problem.

30.   Solve for x.

$$\frac{2x}{x + 3} - \frac{4}{x - 3} = \frac{-6}{x + 3}$$

31.     Prove the following identities:

   (a)     $\sec 2x = \dfrac{\cosec^2 x}{\cosec^2 x - 2}$

   (b)     $\dfrac{\sec x}{\cosec x} = \dfrac{1 + \tan x}{1 + \cot x}$

   (c)     $\sec^2 x + \cosec^2 x = \sec^2 x . \cosec^2 x$

   What values of x are excluded for these identities? (How would you quantify these identities?)

32.     There are three suspects A, B and C for the murder of Mr Peacock. If A had murdered Mr Peacock, he would have been in town. However, it is known that he was not in town at the time of the murder. B either has an alibi or he was framed. However, it is known that B was not framed. If C had murderderd Mr Peacock, the dog would not have barked (since the dog knew him). If the dog did not bark, the neighbours would not be woken. However, it is known that the neighbours awoke. Who murdered Mr Peacock?

# Bibliography

Bailey, C.A.R., 1964: **Sets** and **Logic** 1. Contemporary
School Mathematics (First Series) Edward Arnold,
Gt. Britain.

Bailey, C.A.R., 1964: **Sets** and **Logic** 2. Contemporary
School Mathematics (Second Series), Edward
Arnold, Gt. Britain.

Brand, T.E. & Wade, D.W.M., 1968: **Exercises** 2. Contemporary School Mathematics, Edward Arnold, Gt.
Britain.

De Villiers, M.D., 1985: **Boolean** **Algebra** **at** **School**.
RUMEUS Curriculum Material Series no. 2, Uni-
versity of Stellenbosch, R.S.A.

Kline, M., 1982: **Mathematics:** **The** **Loss** **of** **Certainty**.
Oxford University Press, New York, U.S.A.

Kramer, E.E., 1970: **The** **Nature** **and** **Growth** **of** **Modern**
**Mathematics**. Princeton University Press, Prince-
ton U.S.A.

Lipschutz, S. 1964: **Set** **Theory** **and** **Related** **Topics**.
Schaum's Outline Series, McGraw-Hill, N.Y.,
U.S.A.

Olivier, A.I. 1987: **Equivalence** not **equality,** Unpu-
blished lecture notes of lecture given at the
12th National Convention for Teachers of Mathematics, Physical Science and Biology, July 1987,
Grahamstown.

SMP 1966: **Additional Mathematics** 1. Cambridge University
Press, Gt. Britain, pp. 133-167.

Solow, D. 1984: **Mathematical** Proofs, Dale Seymour Pu-
blications, Palo Alto, U.S.A.

The State Education Department of NY 1977: **Three-year
sequence for High School Mathematics** 1 and 2.
Albany NY, U.S.A.

www.ingramcontent.com/pod-product-compliance
Lightning Source LLC
Chambersburg PA
CBHW062011040426
42447CB00010B/2000